Copyright © 2020 Jean Keow

All rights reserved. No part of this publication can be reproduced, distributed, or transmitted in any form or any means including photography, photocopying, recording, or any other electronic or mechanical means, without prior written permission of the publisher except in the case of brief quotations featured in critical reviews and certain non-commercial uses permitted by the copyright law. For permission, requests write to:

Nuclei Brand Marketing Solutions LLP,-addressed to the Permission Coordinator at the address below:

180 Paya Lebar Road #10-01, Yi Guang Building, Singapore 409032

ISBN: 9798571496469

Imprint: Independently published

Any references to historical events, real names are used fictitiously. Names, characters, and places are products of the author's imagination.

Book illustrators: Lidya Riana (Internal Pages & Back Cover), Roopal Jian (Front Cover)

First Printing Edition: 2020

Published by: Nuclei Brand Marketing Solutions LLP

Website: www.nucleibrandmarketing.com

Now you see me, now you don't

Now you see me, now you don't,
think you can catch me, but you won't.
Camouflage makes me disappear,
as quickly as I reappear.
High or low, right or left,
guess where I've flown?

What am I?

Preface

Parents should start talking about **science** with their children from an early age because **science** is about everything around us. It is natural for children to be curious because they like to explore and discover things. It is all about providing them with the right, fun-filled experience to whet their appetite for learning **science**. In the same vein, parents can also learn from their children's curiosity as every moment spent with our children, or even grandchildren, is precious. My granddaughters, Kate and Christy, inspire me. I thank Kate for her contribution of limericks.

Science is also critical to the improvement of children's reading, writing, and reasoning skills.

In my childhood, I had spent much time with my father through his photography and music hobbies. We connected through this, and he literally opened my eyes to the wonders of the world of **science.**

In this series of **science** books, I aim to energise and empower parents to have fun with their children providing them with remarkable experiences through science adventures.

Take the first step to be your child's "Top Influencer" in **science**-related subject.

WHAT IS SCIENCE?

Science is about discovering the world around us through observing, asking, listening, describing, and experimenting. It encourages us to be curious and adventurous about both Living Things, and Non-Living Things.

Living Things

Things that are alive like people and animals. They move, grow and reproduce. They also need air, water and food.

Non-Living Things

They are not alive. They do not grow, reproduce not need air, food and water.

Once alive

Never alive

LET US MEET KATY AND TESSA!

Katy loves science. She likes being called a 'young scientist'.

Her best friend, Tessa, shares the same interest.

Katy has many adventure-filled stories that show how science works in our daily lives. She is happy to share them with you!

ADVENTURES WITH LIVING THINGS

OUR AMAZING PLAYGROUND

One of Katy's and Tessa's favourite playgrounds is located at Singapore's Upper Seletar Reservoir. In the mornings, they can hear the humming noise of the aeroplanes at the nearby airbase. They can also hear the rippling sound of water.

The reflection of clouds on the surface of the water makes such a beautiful sight. Butterflies and dragonflies fly merrily among the bushes. Katy and Tessa can see grasshoppers chomping on the juicy blades of grass.

On one of their visits, Tessa sees a fish trapped amongst the rocks. It must have been swept up to the rocks during high tide. Tessa sees a red spot on the fish's tail and thinks that it is bleeding. She shouts to Katy to get help. Katy's grandfather runs over and tries to catch the fish with his bare hands. But the fish is slippery, and it falls back into the water. It cannot swim into the open reservoir because its path is blocked.

Then Katy's grandfather takes out a recyclable sunglasses pouch from his pocket. He covers one hand with the pouch and lifts the fish from the rocks into a shallow waterway. Soon the fish makes its way to the open reservoir. Katy, Tessa, and Katy's grandfather can see the fish with a spotted red tail swimming hurriedly away. Katy and Tessa say that rescuing the trapped fish is their good deed for the day.

Katy's Lesson on the Life Cycles of Animals

The different animal groups all reproduce to ensure their survival. The life cycles of animals tell us about the continuous growth process of their young to adulthood. The life cycle of animals is either a three-stage or a four-stage one. Here are some examples to look at.

The Life Cycle of the Butterfly

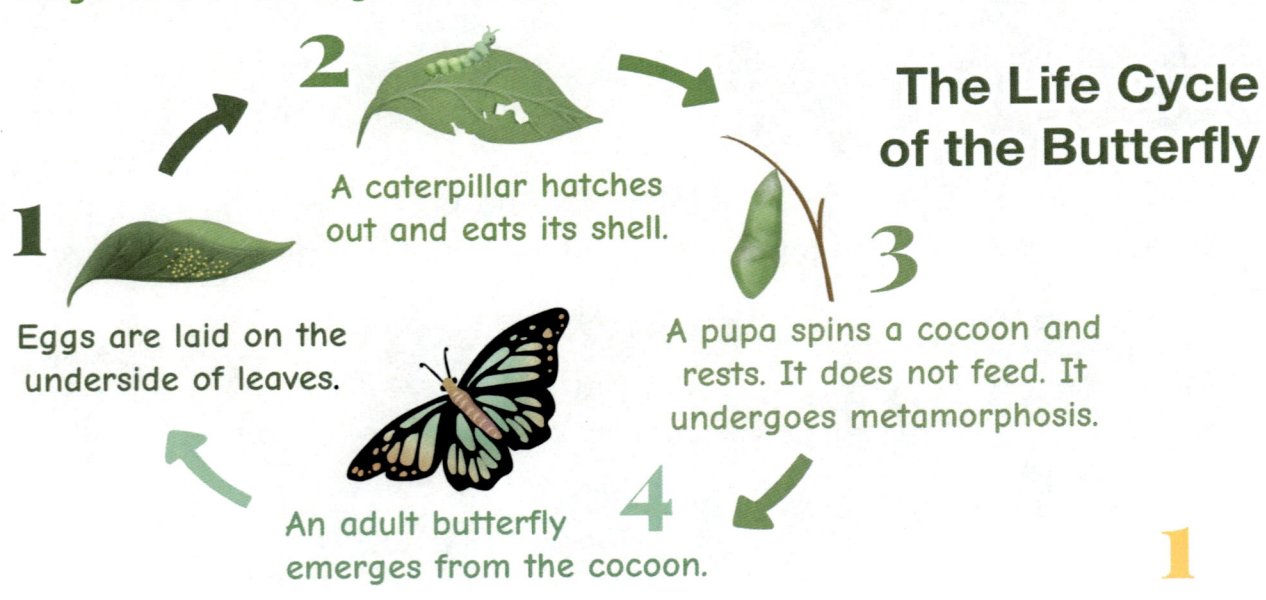

1. Eggs are laid on the underside of leaves.
2. A caterpillar hatches out and eats its shell.
3. A pupa spins a cocoon and rests. It does not feed. It undergoes metamorphosis.
4. An adult butterfly emerges from the cocoon.

The Life Cycle of the Grasshopper

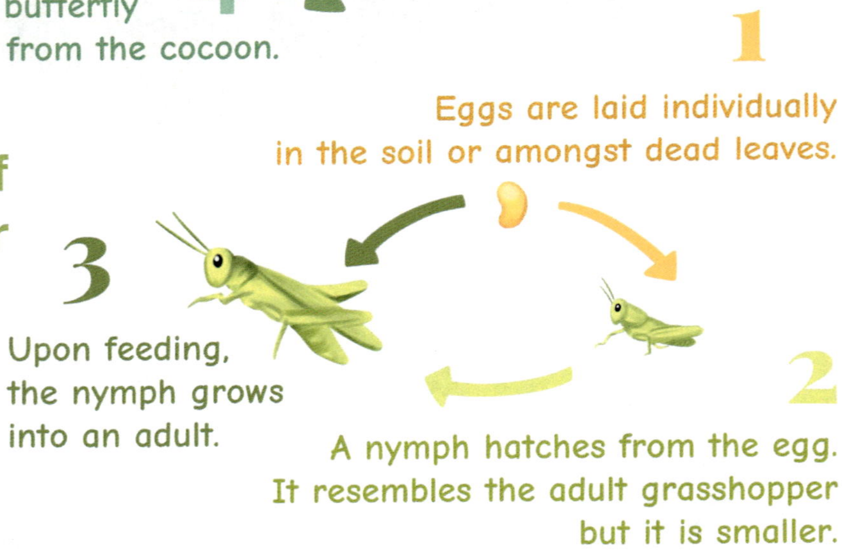

1. Eggs are laid individually in the soil or amongst dead leaves.
2. A nymph hatches from the egg. It resembles the adult grasshopper but it is smaller.
3. Upon feeding, the nymph grows into an adult.

The Life Cycle of the Chicken

1. Adult Chicken.
2. Egg - A fertilised egg that is incubated by the hen.
3. Chick – A young chick that is fed by the adult chicken.

Katy's Walking on Eggs Experiment!

❓ Aim: To walk on eggs without breaking them.

Eggs are stronger than you think! Do you know that you can walk on eggs without breaking them? The secret is in the shape of the egg. Eggs are strongest at the top and bottom. The curve of the egg helps to distribute pressure evenly. Pressure is dependent on area. The bigger the area, the smaller the pressure. Have you tried to walk on eggs? A few things can affect how successful you will be. The first thing is to make sure that your weight is distributed evenly. You do this by placing your feet as flat as possible on the eggs.

METHOD
👉 Lay some newspaper on the ground. On top of this place three trays of eggs in a row. Each tray should have 30 eggs.

👉 Remove your shoes and walk over the eggs.

Make sure that you do not put pressure on your heels or toes when you walk over the eggs. Otherwise you will reduce the area of contact and increase pressure on the eggs at your heels or toes. Weight also plays an important role. The heavier the person, the more likely will the eggs break. Katy and Tessa have invited two friends, Satish and Nahar, to join them. Katy's grandfather has decided to give it a try, too. They have so much fun and a good laugh when they hear the eggs cracking under Katy's grandfather's feet!

Katy's Aquarium Surprise!

On Katy's birthday, she finds a big gift right outside her bedroom door. She tears off the wrapping paper and finds a box inside, with the words 'AQUARIUM' on it. Katy jumps for joy at this wonderful surprise. It is just what she wanted. Immediately, Katy asks if they can go to buy fish and accessories at the local fish farm over the weekend. Mummy and Daddy suggest that Tessa comes with them.

The following Saturday, the two girls set off with Katy's parents to the fish farm. Katy and Tessa buy an assortment of tropical fish such as Guppies, Swordtails, Angel Fish and a Sucker Fish. The Sucker Fish is used to clean up the algae that grows inside fish tanks. Katy and Tessa also buy a pump for the tank as well as a background of water plants, pebbles, shells, floating sea horses, water plants, a fish net and fish food.

When Katy and Tessa go back to Katy's house, they spend the whole afternoon assembling and setting up the tank. Once they are done, they sit in front of the aquarium. They reward themselves with a bowl of ice-cream for their hard work. Katy and Tessa enjoy the rest of the day relaxing and watching the fish swimming about in the pretty tank.

MORE ABOUT FISH

Some fish lay eggs, but others give birth to their young alive. The Angel Fish usually lays eggs on a broad leaf of a water plant. The eggs hatch after about 60 hours and then the fries are in the wriggler stage for about 5 days.

Guppies and Swordtails give birth to live young instead of laying eggs. They give birth to more than 20 fries at a time. But if you do not separate the adults from the fries, they eat their own young. The adult fish thinks that the small wriggly fries are food.

Katy's Fish Hatchery Experiment

? Aim To use a fish hatchery to separate the pregnant adult Guppy from her fries after birth.

1 Purchase a simple plastic fish hatchery and assemble it.

2 Attach the fish hatchery, with the plastic suction pads provided, to a corner of your aquarium.

3 Place your pregnant guppy in the upper chamber and wait.

OBSERVATION
When the Guppy gives birth to her fries, the fries are forced through the slits in the hatchery divider. But the adult Guppy is too big to go through the slits.

CONCLUSION
The fries has been safely separated from the adult Guppy in the fish hatchery.

ADVENTURES WITH NON-LIVING THINGS

DRAW AWAY!

On wet and rainy days, Katy and Tessa like to spend their time drawing with the help of YouTube tutorials. They draw pictures of animals, cartoon characters and food! Katy and Tessa learn a lot from their drawing sessions. They know that it is important to have the right drawing tools. They each have their own set of pencils for sketching, a set of colour pencils for colouring, an eraser and a sharpener.

Katy and Tessa find that the pencil is an amazing drawing tool. The pencil can bring their characters to life, and give shape to your imagination. Katy's Mummy told them that pencils are made up of pencil leads and wood. Pencil leads are made from a material called graphite. Katy and Tessa enjoy adding colour to their drawings. Colour pencils are not made of graphite. The cores of colour pencils are made from wax and colour pigments.

Katy's Mummy helps the girls laminate their two favourite drawings. They each punch a hole in one end of their drawing and tie a ribbon though it. Katy and Tessa can now use them as bookmarks. They think these bookmarks will make great gifts for their friends, too.

Do you know that **graphite** and **diamond** are of the same **carbon** family?

An element like carbon (C) can exist in different structures. The structure of graphite consists of layers or sheets of carbon (C) atoms that can slide easily. So, when the pencil lead is drawn across a piece of paper, a mark is left behind.

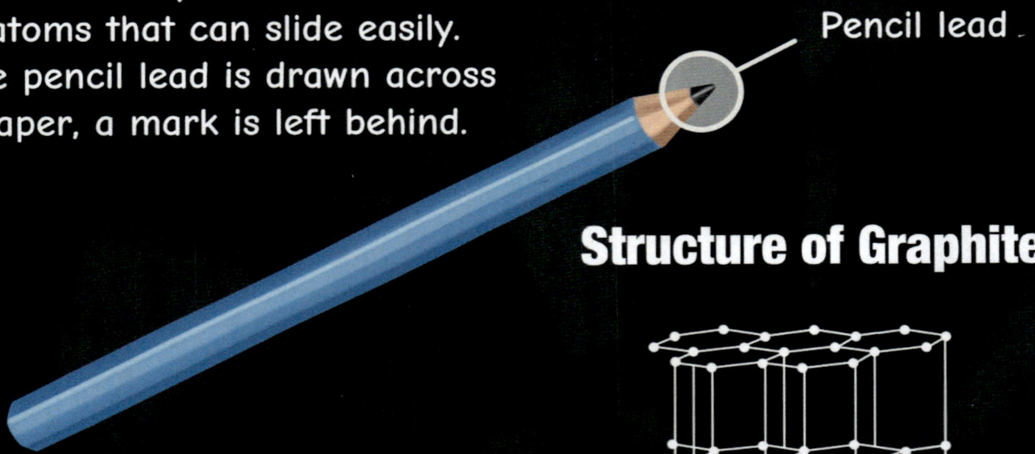

Pencil lead

Structure of Graphite

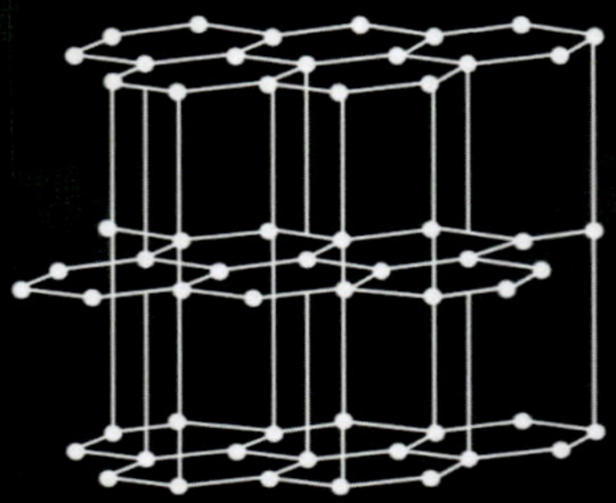

Structure of Diamond

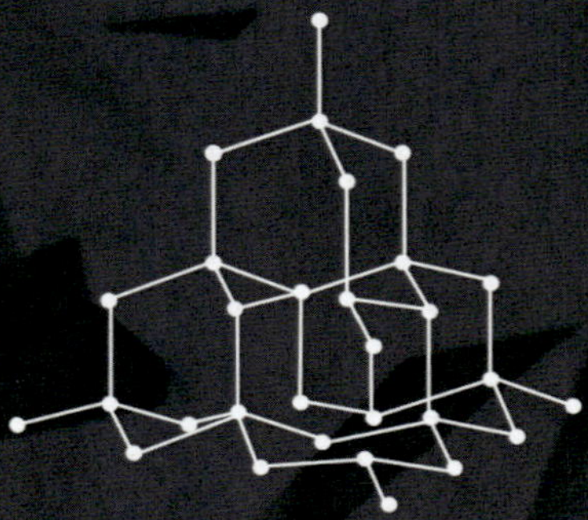

Diamonds are also made up of carbon (C) atoms. They are formed by high heat and pressure deep in the earth. They are brought to the earth's surface during volcanic eruptions.

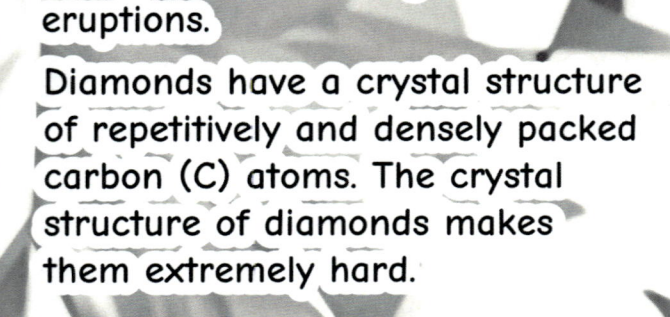

Diamonds have a crystal structure of repetitively and densely packed carbon (C) atoms. The crystal structure of diamonds makes them extremely hard.

Katy Makes Rock Candy by Growing Sugar Crystals Experiment

Adult supervision required!

? Aim To make rock candy by growing sugar crystals.

A crystal is a solid with atoms and molecules arranged in a repeated pattern, creating geometrical shapes. Examples of crystals are that of salt and sugar. Katy and Tessa make their own Rock Candy by growing sugar crystals.

1 350ml of water
Place 350ml of water in pot over an electrical hob.

2 1kg of sugar
Slowly add in 1kg Sugar. Stir the sugar until it has completely melted.

3 4 hours
Cool the saturated sugar solution for 4 hours.

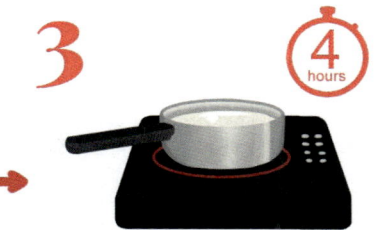

4 Pour the cooled, saturated sugar solution into 3 glasses. Add food colouring and flavour essence into each of the 3 glasses. Stir well.

5 Dip half the wooden stick in the saturated sugar solution. Then coat one end of the wooden stick with sugar.

6 Suspend the wooden stick with a cloth peg or plastic clip and place the sugar-coated stick into the coloured sugar solution. Repeat this with 2 other sticks.

7 2 weeks
Grow the sugar crystals over a period of 2 weeks. Use the stem of a tablespoon to remove the big sugar crystal. Each stick is now a delicious Rock Candy.

8 Dry each stick of Rock Candy for 30 minutes on a plate.

OBSERVATION & CONCLUSION
The saturated sugar solutions have solidified into crystals and grown.

Birthday Games: First a Treasure Hunt then a Car Race!

Katy is looking forward to her 8th birthday party. She has planned a picnic at her neighbourhood playground. Katy's Mummy has prepared sandwiches, cupcakes, Jelly Hearts, and lemonade. Katy has invited Tessa and her neighbours Satish, Sumitar, Nahar, Matt and Justin. Treasure Hunt is one of Katy's favourite party games. Katy decides to give the game a little twist. Katy's Mummy packs a compass into each goodie bag for the children who are invited to Katy's birthday party.

KATY'S TREASURE HUNT GAME

Katy draws a treasure map and gives clues to the locations of the 'hidden treasures' by providing her friends with directions. Katy's directions are North, South, East, West, North-East, North-West, South-East and South-West. The children use their compasses and manage to uncover the hidden treasures in their neighbourhood playground. It is such fun and Tessa finds the most hidden treasures.

271°W

Katy's 'Minute to win it' race!

At Katy's birthday party, she has a toy car racing game. She gives her friends each a toy racing car with a button magnet taped on top of it. They are also given an ice-cream stick with a button magnet taped on one end of the stick. The children use the magnets on the ice-cream stick to move their cars along the racing lanes, placed on the jogging track.

Magnetic force can act from a distance. But there is a limit to how far the magnet can be from the magnetic object. The children learn that they need to keep their magnets close to their toy racing cars. Each child has one minute to move their toy car with the magnet on the ice-cream stick. The toy car that moves the farthest in one minute wins. It is an exciting race. Katy and her friends have a great time. Satish wins the first prize! He receives a medal and a box of chocolates.

LET'S TALK ABOUT MAGNETS

A magnet has a magnetic field that attracts magnetic materials. A natural magnet is called a lodestone which is a piece of iron ore. The Earth is a big magnet. All the north poles of magnets will point to the Earth's magnetic north pole and all the south poles will point to the earth's magnetic south pole.

Magnetic North Pole

Geographic North Pole

Geographic South Pole

Magnetic South Pole

It is interesting to note that a freely suspended magnet always comes to rest in the N-S direction.

Man-made magnets are made of steel or iron. Magnets can come in different shapes and sizes. We can have the bar magnet, the U-shaped magnet, the button magnet, and a ring magnet. Magnets can also be used to drive motion.

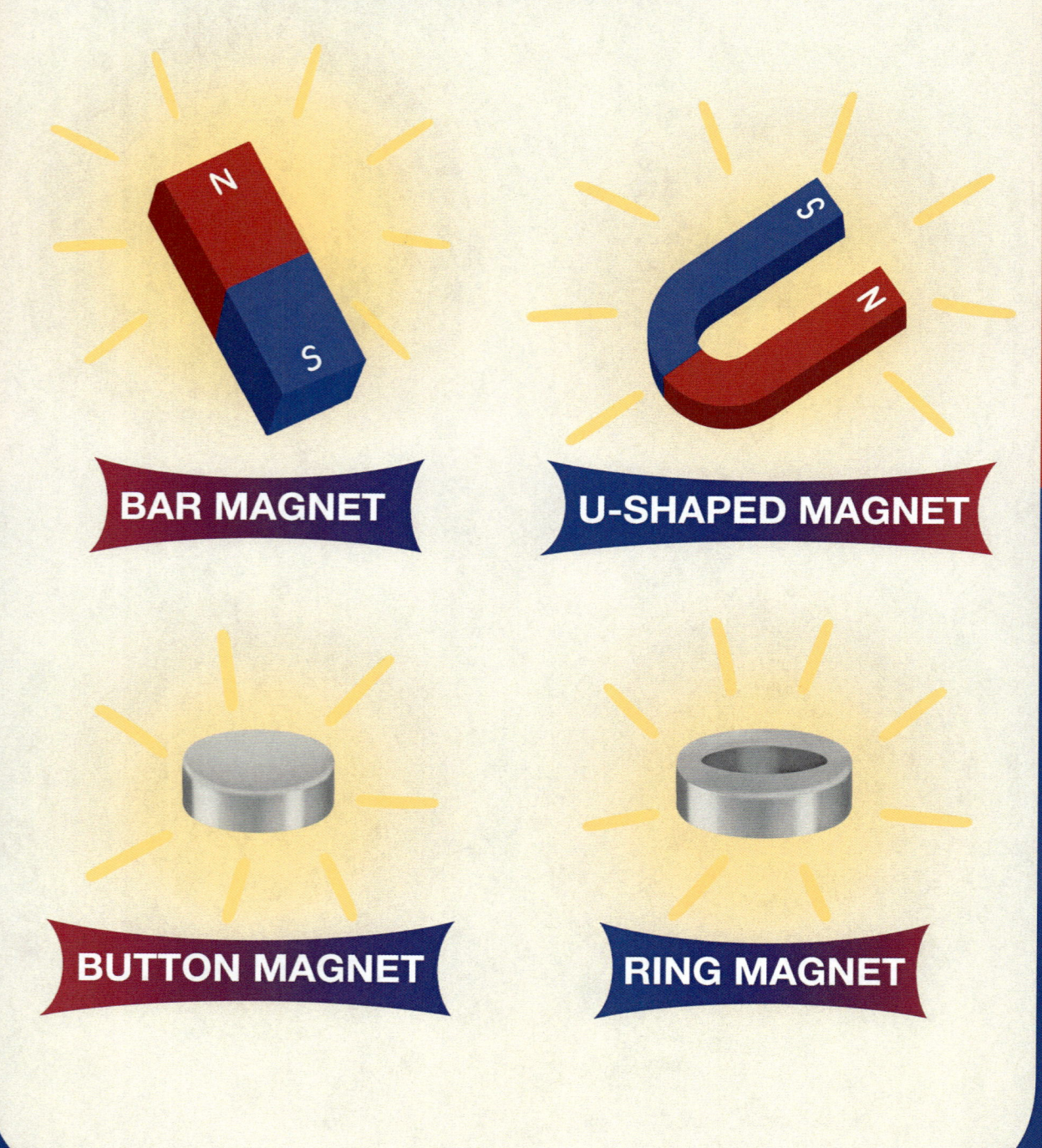

BAR MAGNET

U-SHAPED MAGNET

BUTTON MAGNET

RING MAGNET

Katy's Temporary Magnet Experiment

? Aim To make a temporary magnet with electricity.

Things you need:
1) An iron nail
2) Wire
3) Two 1.5V C Batteries

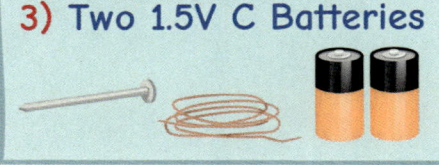

1 Coil wire around your iron nail.

2 Attach each end of the wire to the battery as shown in the illustration below.

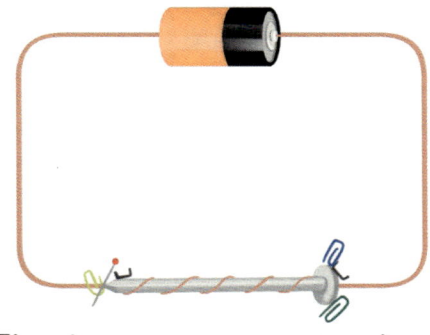

The temporary magnet can attract magnetic objects like paper clips, staples and pins.

3 Increase the number of turns of the coil and repeat the experiment.

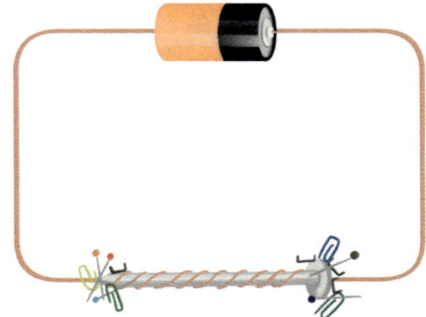

4 Increase the amount of electricity passing through the iron nail by using 2 batteries.

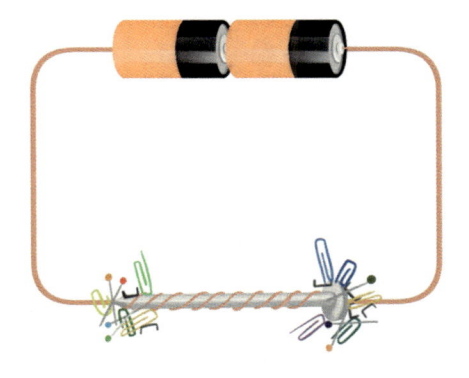

OBSERVATION & CONCLUSION

1) The iron nail behaves like a magnet when electricity passes through it. When the iron nail is disconnected from the battery, it has no magnetic strength.
2) As the number of coils increases, the magnetic strength of the temporary magnet increases.
3) As the amount of electricity that passes through increases, the magnetic strength increases.

What's HOT? HOT? HOT? Solar Energy!

One sunny Sunday morning, Katy thinks it will be great to bake cookies in a homemade solar oven. She asks Tessa to join her. Katy's Mummy ordered pizza for lunch the day before and the girls use the pizza box to make their solar oven. Katy and Tessa make some cookie dough. For comparison, they also bake some cookies in the electric oven. Later in the morning, the sky turns cloudy. It takes 5 hours for the cookie dough in the solar oven to change in texture. This takes much longer than what Katy and Tessa expected. The cookies look pale and unappetizing.

Cookie baked with solar oven

Cookie baked with an electric oven

Katy and Tessa are glad that they also baked cookies in the electric oven. They eat these at tea-time with their ice-cold chocolate drink. The electric oven cookies are simply delicious.

MORE ABOUT SOLAR ENERGY

Inverter

Fuse box

Today, solar energy is a hot topic. Solar energy is energy from the sun. Other sources of energy are from coal, oil, and natural gases. These sources are not renewable. The sun is a mass of flaming gases and it gives off lots of energy. Solar energy is renewable. Other renewable resources are water and wind.

How can we harness solar energy? We can make use of solar panels to capture solar energy. Singapore is near the equator and here, we can make greater use of solar energy. Katy saw on the news that Singapore is aiming to power 350,000 homes with solar energy by the year 2030. Solar panels are made up of solar cells. Solar cells have several layers as seen in the diagram below.

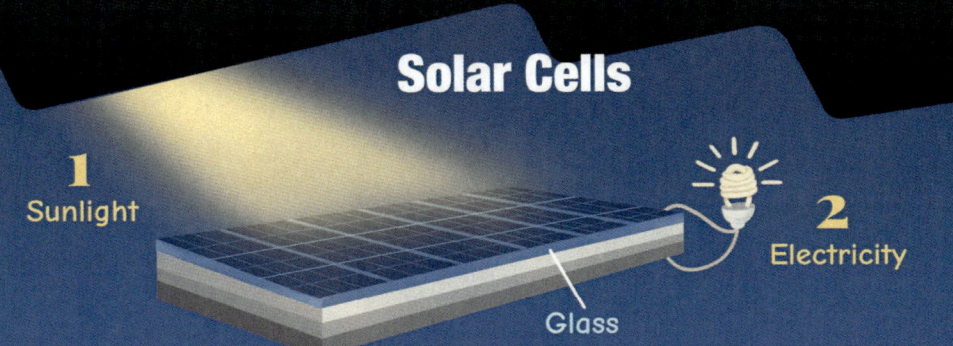

Solar Cells

1 Sunlight

2 Electricity

Glass

The first layer of glass allows the light to pass through.

Katy's Baking Experiment using Solar Energy!

? Aim To bake cookies in a homemade solar oven.

What you need

- A pizza box
- Some aluminium foil
- Some plastic wrap
- A sheet of black art paper
- A long chopstick
- Double-sided tape

1 Cover the bottom flap of the pizza box with a sheet of aluminium foil using double-sided tape.

2 Line the inner sides of the box with aluminium foil.

3 Place the black art paper at the bottom of the pizza box and taped a sheet of aluminium foil on top of the black art paper.

black art paper

4 Place your cut cookie dough into the pizza box and cover the opening of the pizza box with a plastic wrap. Use a chopstick to prop up the flap of the pizza box.

plastic warp

OBSERVATION
It took 5 hours to cook the cookies because it turned cloudy on the Sunday morning. On a sunny day, it probably would have taken about half the time.

CONCLUSION
The more heat is trapped in the solar oven, the faster the cookies will cook.

Katy's ABCs of SCIENCE:

A is for **_Allotropes_**. The same element such as Carbon can have different structural forms. Graphite and Diamond are both allotropes of Carbon.	**E** is for **_Energy_**. Energy is the ability to do work and is related to distance and time. Energy cannot be created nor destroyed but changes from one form to another. There are different types of energy like Light Energy, Heat, Electrical Energy, Magnetic Energy, Nuclear Energy, Kinetic Energy, Potential Energy etc.
B is for **_Battery._** Battery is a cell that contains chemical energy. A battery produces electrical energy using different metals in a chemical solution.	**F** is for **_Freezing_**. It is when liquids turn into solids like water into ice. There are three (3) states of matter. This means that matter can exist as a solid, a liquid and a gas.
C is for **_Chemistry_**. Chemistry is a branch of science involving non-living things. Chemistry studies about chemical substances and their characteristics, behaviour, and changes during a reaction with other chemical substances.	**G** is for **_Gravity._** It is an invisible force that pulls a body to the earth. It was discovered by Sir Isaac Newton. The moon rotates round the earth because of gravitational force.
D is for **_Dissolve._** When a solid like Salt or Sugar disappears when stirred in water. It is said that it has dissolved in water. *"Like dissolves like".* This means compounds that are from the same family of the periodic table will dissolve each other.	**H** is for **_Heat._** Heat is a form of energy that is transferred due to a difference in temperature. Heat Energy flows from a hotter object to a cooler object.

I is for ***Invertebrate.*** An invertebrate refers to an animal that does not have a backbone. Examples are earthworm, a sea urchin, and a spider.	**M** is for ***Mass***. Mass is the amount of substance in a thing or matter. The mass of an object remains the same, but its weight changes from place to place. We are weightless in space.
J is for ***Joints***. Joints in bones are used to connect two bones to enable movement. Joints give flexibility. The ball and socket joint can be found in the hips and shoulders.	**N** is for ***Neutron***. A neutron is part of the nucleus of an atom. There are electrons circulating around the nucleus. The nucleus is made up of neutrons and protons. The neutrons and protons are bound together by enclosed energy. Neutrons have no charge.
K is for ***Kinetic.*** It is related to movement. Kinetic energy is the energy of a moving object. The kinetic energy of an object is related to its mass and speed. For an object with the same mass, the one with greater speed will have greater kinetic energy as in a rolling ball.	**P** is for ***Poles.*** Here we are referring to Magnetic Poles. Poles refer to the two (2) regions of the magnets with high magnetic strength or power. They are the North Pole and South Pole. Like-poles repel and unlike Poles attract.
L is for ***Light***. Light is a form of energy and it allows us to see. The main source of light is the sun. Other artificial light sources are a torch, a burning candle, or a light bulb. Light travels in a straight line.	**Q** is for ***Quartz***. Quartz is a hard mineral found in sand and gravel. Quartz is in the form of a crystal. Quartz is used in electronics to convert mechanical energy to an electrical signal. Quartz can also convert digital electrical signal into mechanical movement.

R is for _Root_. Root is a part of a plant. Roots of plants are usually found underground and are used to draw water and minerals from the oil. But there are roots like that of the air plant or Banyan tree that are above ground. These roots are aerial roots and are used for breathing or clasping.	**V is for _Vacuum_.** Vacuum refers to a space that does not contain any form of matter. There is no air in a vacuum. No living things can live in a vacuum.
S is for _Solution_. A solution is a liquid in which a solid or gas has been dissolved. The dissolved substance (solid or gas) is called the solute. The liquid used to dissolve the solute is called the solvent. Solution does not change into new substances.	**W is for _Weight_.** Weight refers to the force of gravity on an object. Weight is different from mass. The weight of an object differs at different places. We are weightless in space because there is no force of gravity.
T is for _Transpiration_. Transpiration is a process where plants lose water. Water is lost as water vapour to the surrounding. The water vapour is lost through evaporation through the leaves of the plants. Transpiration helps to cool the plants.	**X is for _X-rays_.** X-rays are enormously powerful waves of energy that can go through substances that light cannot. X-rays can be used to make pictures that show the inside of an object or human body. X-rays are strong radiation and can damage or destroy body cells. You must be properly shielded or protected in its presence.

U is for **_Units._** There are different units used in measurement. There are two types of measuring systems. The Metric and Imperial systems. The metric units of length or distance are millimetre (mm), centimetre (cm), metre (m) and kilometre (km). The Imperial units of length or distance are inches (ins), feet (ft), yard (yd) and miles.

Y is for **_Yeast._** Yeast is a living single cell organism. There are approximately 1500 types of yeast.
Active dry yeast used in our kitchen can multiply with sugar and water.

Z is for **_Zero._** In Physics, an absolute zero temperature is impossible to reach temperature equivalent to minus 273C or degree Celsius or minus 460 F or degree Fahrenheit. All atoms will cease to move.

Use Katy's ABCs Of Science for WORD SEARCH

```
L X M C S R E I O K T M W M W
S M R R O O N N Z Q R A E H V
K P Q A H O E V E F A S I E A
Y D U T Y T R E R R N S G A L
E I A C B S G R O E S Q H T L
A S R H A M Y T G E P S T J O
S S T E T S U E R Z I K L O T
T O Z M T O U B A I R I X I R
V L Y I E L N R V N A N V N O
J V L S R U I A I G T E A T P
U E I T Y T T T O I T C S E
C Q G R Q I S E Y L O I U I S
G L H Y M O H J I X N C U M F
G C T I V N E U T R O N M F X
K L Z W R P O L E S I W U D T
```

Made in the USA
Monee, IL
08 November 2022